Mein Sprachenportfolio
Klasse 4

My name is _____.

I'm in class _____ at _____.

**So habe ich
im Englischunterricht gearbeitet:**

	1. Halbjahr	2. Halbjahr
Ich habe aufmerksam zugehört.		
Ich habe mich regelmäßig gemeldet.		
Ich habe versucht, neue Wörter genau nachzusprechen.		
Ich habe versucht, in Gesprächen möglichst viel auf Englisch zu sagen.		
Ich habe die Lieder mitgesungen.		
Ich habe mindestens einen Reim gründlich geübt und aufgesagt.		
Ich habe bei den Hörübungen genau zugehört.		
Ich konnte verstehen, was meine Lehrerin / mein Lehrer auf Englisch sagt.		
Ich habe Wörter richtig abgeschrieben.		
Ich konnte schon kleine Texte schreiben.		

Das kann ich schon

Diese Nomen kenne ich:
Schreibe 10 bis 15 Nomen auf, die für dich besonders wichtig sind.

Diese Verben kenne ich:

Weitere Wörter, die ich oft benutzt und mir gut gemerkt habe:

Das möchte ich im 4. Schuljahr lernen:

three 3

Back to school

1 **Diese Zahlen kann ich aufschreiben:**
Hilfe findest du im Activity Book auf Seite 3.

10	30	40	80	90
___	___	___	___	___

20	50	60	70	100
___	___	___	___	___

2 **Ich kann jemanden nach der Uhrzeit fragen:**

_____, please?

3 **Ich kann sagen, wie spät es ist:**

 It's _____.

 _____.

 It's quarter to eight.

4 Das kann ich auch schon auf Englisch:

Ich kann den Rap „Welcome back to school" mitsprechen.

Ich konnte viele Aufgaben des Spiels im Pupil's Book richtig lösen.

Ich kann das Lied „100 little kangaroos are sitting on Big Ben" singen.

4 four

At home

1 ✏️ **Diese Räume kann ich benennen und aufschreiben:**
Hilfe findest du im Activity Book auf Seite 6.

 _____   _____   _____

 _____  _____

2 ✂️ **Ich kenne diese Möbelstücke:**
Male oder klebe sie auf. Schreibe das englische Wort dazu.

3 ✏️ **Ich kann sagen, ob etwas zu groß, zu klein oder genau richtig ist:**
Hilfe findest du im Activity Book auf Seite 7 und im Pupil's Book auf Seite 8.

The chair is _____.

The bed is _____.

The wardrobe is _____.

4 **Das hat mir geholfen, die Geschichte „Gavin the ghost" zu verstehen:**

_____
_____

Let's have lunch

1. Für mein Lieblingssandwich brauche ich:
Hilfe findest du im Activity Book auf Seite 8 und im Pupil's Book auf Seite 9.

_____

_____

_____

2. Diese Gegenstände kann ich benennen und aufschreiben:
Hilfe findest du im Activity Book auf Seite 10.

_____

_____

_____

3. Das kann ich auch schon auf Englisch:

Ich kenne verschiedene Mittagsgerichte.

Ich habe verstanden, was Phil und Emily bestellt haben.

Ich kann selbst etwas zum Essen oder Trinken bestellen.

Ich kann den „Sandwich Rap" mitsingen.

4. So habe ich eine Strophe des „Sandwich Rap" auswendig geübt:

_____

_____

Hobbies and sports

1 ✏ Diese Hobbys kann ich benennen und aufschreiben:
Hilfe findest du im Activity Book auf Seite 12.

_____

 _____

_____ _____

 _____

My hobby is _____.

2 Das kann ich auch schon auf Englisch:

Ich kann einen Steckbrief über mich und meine Hobbys schreiben.

Ich habe das Interview mit Dirk Nowitzki gehört und verstanden. ○ ○ ○

Ich habe selbst ein Interview gemacht und als Rollenspiel vorgeführt. ○ ○ ○

Ich kann den „Sporty Rap" mitsprechen. ○ ○ ○

3 Feedback

Das hat mir in dieser Unit am meisten Spaß gemacht:
_____
_____

Das hat mir nicht gefallen:
_____
_____

seven **7**

My day

1 ✏️ **Ich kann sagen, was ich im Tagesverlauf mache:**
Hilfe findest du im Activity Book auf den Seiten 16 und 17 und im Pupil's Book auf Seite 13.

Today is _____.

At _____ in the morning I _____.

At _____.

At _____ in the afternoon I _____.

At _____ in the evening I _____.

At _____.

> go to bed   read a book   have lunch   go to school
> go home   have breakfast   do my homework   watch TV

2 Das kann ich auch schon auf Englisch:

Ich kann die Geschichte „Emily's day" verstehen.

Ich kann das Lied „Through the day" singen.

Ich habe die Bilder zur Geschichte von Alpha 72 zugeordnet und die fehlenden Wörter eingetragen.

Ich kann die Geschichte „At the same time" verstehen und ein Minibuch dazu basteln.

3 ✏️ **Das sind meine Lieblingssätze aus „At the same time":**

_____
_____
_____

8 eight

Shopping

1 ✏️ **Ich kann viele Dinge benennen und aufschreiben, die man im Supermarkt kaufen kann:**
Hilfe findest du im Activity Book auf Seite 18 und im Pupil's Book auf Seite 15.

2 So bin ich mit schwierigen Wörtern beim Lesen der Geschichte „Something good" umgegangen: ✓

☐ Ich habe Wörter im Wörterbuch nachgeschlagen.

☐ Ich konnte mir die Bedeutung einiger Wörter aus dem Zusammenhang der Geschichte selbst erklären.

☐ Ich habe mir Wörter deutlich vorsprechen lassen.

☐ Ich habe den Text mehrmals von der CD gehört.

☐ Ich habe meine/n Lehrer/in oder Mitschüler gefragt.

☐ _____

Shopping

3 ✏️ **Ich kann die Geschäfte in einem Einkaufszentrum benennen:**
Hilfe findest du im Activity Book auf den Seiten 20 und 21.

_____   _____

_____   _____

_____   _____

_____   _____

4 Das kann ich auch schon auf Englisch:

Ich kann verstehen, was Emily, Liz, Eric und Phil im Supermarkt einkaufen.

Ich kann sagen, auf welcher Etage des Einkaufszentrums ein Geschäft ist.

Ich kann den Hörtext von Liz und Phil im Kleidungsgeschäft verstehen. ○ ○ ○

Ich kann mit einem Partner ein Verkaufsgespräch vorspielen.

10 ten

Jack and the beanstalk

1 ✎ **Diese Wörter kann ich benennen und aufschreiben:**
Hilfe findest du im Activity Book auf Seite 23 und im Pupil's Book auf Seite 18.

_____ _____ _____ _____

| beans   cow   pie   giant |

2 ✎ **Ich kann die Sätze lesen und in der richtigen Reihenfolge nummerieren:**

☐ During the night the beans grow and grow.

☐ Jack takes the gold and runs away.

☐ We must sell the cow.

☐ Fee, fi, foe, fum, I smell the blood of an Englishman.

☐ Jack climbs up the beanstalk.

3 **So habe ich geübt, den Text zu lesen:**

_____

_____

4 **Feedback**

Das hat mir in dieser Unit am meisten Spaß gemacht:

_____

Das hat mir nicht gefallen:

_____

eleven **11**

Transport

1 ✏️ **Diese Wörter kann ich benennen und aufschreiben:**
Hilfe findest du im Pupil's Book auf Seite 20.

_____   _____   _____

_____   _____   _____

Ich kenne auch noch diese Fortbewegungsmittel:

_____

 _____

2 **Ich kann die Geschichte „Detective Brighthead" verstehen.**

Diese Verkehrsmittel kommen in der Geschichte vor:

_____

3 ✏️ **Das kann ich auch schon auf Englisch:**
Hilfe findest du im Activity Book auf Seite 26.

Ich kann jemandem sagen, wie man von der London Bridge nach Wimbledon kommt:

_____

Ich kann fragen, wie ich zum London Eye komme:

_____

Wild animals

1 ✏️ **Diese Tiere kann ich benennen und aufschreiben:**
Hilfe findest du im Activity Book auf Seite 27.

_____ _____ _____ _____

_____ _____ _____ _____

2 ✏️ **Ich kann sagen und aufschreiben, wie die Tiere sind:**
Hilfe findest du im Activity Book auf Seite 29.

The hippo is _____ .   The giraffe is _____ .

The snake is _____ .   The tortoise is _____ .

The lion is _____ .   The monkey is _____ .

3 ✏️ **Ich kann das Tier-Rätsel lösen:**

It's grey and very big.
It has got four legs and a trunk.
It lives in the jungle.
It eats leaves and grass.

It's an _____ .

4 ✏️ **Ich kann selbst ein Tier-Rätsel aufschreiben:**

_____
_____

It's _____ .

Wild animals

5 **Das hat mir geholfen, die Geschichte „The clever tortoise"
zu verstehen:** ✓

☐ Ich habe mir vorgestellt, was in der Geschichte passiert.

☐ Ich habe mir die Bilder im Pupil's Book angesehen.

☐ Ich habe den Text in den Sprechblasen mitgelesen.

☐ Ich habe beim Hören auf Wörter geachtet, die ich schon kenne.

6 **Das kann ich auch schon auf Englisch:**

Ich kann das Lied „Walking through the jungle" singen.

Ich kann den Reim „Five little monkeys" mitsprechen.

Ich kann mein Tier-Rätsel vortragen.

7 **Feedback**

Das hat mir in dieser Unit am meisten Spaß gemacht:

_____

_____

Das hat mir nicht gefallen und das fand ich schwierig:

_____

_____

At the doctor's

1 ✏️ **Diese Wörter kann ich benennen und aufschreiben:**
Hilfe findest du im Activity Book auf Seite 30.

headache   earache
backache   neckache

2 ✏️ **Ich kann sagen, wenn mir etwas weh tut:**
Hilfe findest du im Activity Book auf Seite 30.

_____

_____

3 ✏️ **Ich weiß, was man bei bestimmten Verletzungen tun muss:**
Hilfe findest du im Pupil's Book auf Seite 29.

_____

_____

Diese Telefonnummer rufe ich im Notfall an: _____

4 **Das kann ich auch schon auf Englisch:**

Ich kann das Lied „The Hokey Cokey" mitsingen
und die Bewegungen dazu machen.

Ich kann den Comic „At the doctor's" verstehen und weiß,   ◯ ◯ ◯
warum alle Tiere aus dem Behandlungszimmer fliehen.

Ich kann die Geschichte „The inline skating accident" verstehen.   ◯ ◯ ◯

fifteen **15**

Going to Scotland

1 ✏️ **Diese Dinge kann ich benennen und aufschreiben:**
Hilfe findest du im Activity Book auf Seite 33 und im Pupil's Book auf Seite 31.

_____   _____   _____

_____   _____   _____

2 Das kann ich auch schon auf Englisch:

Ich kann die Geschichte „Sally and the Loch Ness Monster" verstehen.

Ich kann sagen, was sich die Familie Brown in Schottland ansehen will.

3 ✏️ **Das weiß ich jetzt über Schottland:**
Hier ist Platz für deine Ideen. Du kannst alles aufschreiben, was du weißt, Bilder aus Prospekten einkleben und beschriften usw.

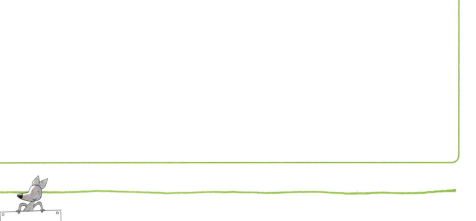

Jobs

1 ✏️ **Diese Berufe kann ich benennen und aufschreiben:**
Hilfe findest du im Activity Book auf Seite 34 und im Pupil's Book auf Seite 33.

_____ _____ _____

_____ _____ _____

2 ✏️ **Das sind meine Eltern, Verwandte oder Bekannte von Beruf:**

My _____ is a _____

_____

_____

3 ✏️ **Das kann ich auch schon auf Englisch:**
Hilfe findest du im Pupil's Book auf Seite 33.

Ich kann andere Kinder fragen, was sie werden wollen:

_____

Ich kann sagen, was ich werden will:

_____

4 **Diese Aufgaben erledige ich zu Hause:**
Hilfe findest du im Pupil's Book auf Seite 34 und im Activity Book auf Seite 35.

I have to _____

_____

Meeting people

1 **Diesen Flaggen kann ich eine Sprache zuordnen:**
Hilfe findest du im Pupil's Book auf Seite 36.

_____ _____ _____

_____ _____ _____

2 Das kann ich auch schon auf Englisch:

Ich kann das Lied „We all live in the same world" singen.

Ich kann einen Freund oder eine Freundin beschreiben.

Das sind die drei wichtigsten Wörter, die ich dazu verwendet habe:

_____

3 **Das hat mir geholfen, unbekannte Wörter in der Geschichte „A rainbow of friends" zu verstehen:** ✓

☐ Ich habe mir die Bilder im Pupil's Book angesehen.

☐ Ich habe mir das Wort aus dem Zusammenhang erschlossen.

☐ Ich kenne ein ähnlich klingendes Wort in einer anderen Sprache.

☐ _____

4 **Diesen Dialog aus dem Activity Book habe ich mir gemerkt, weil er mir besonders wichtig ist:**

_____

_____

Guy Fawkes

1 **Diese Wörter kann ich benennen und aufschreiben:**
Hilfe findest du im Activity Book auf den Seiten 38 und 39 und im Pupil's Book auf Seite 37.

_____   _____

_____   _____   _____

2 Das kann ich auch schon auf Englisch:

Ich kann die Geschichte von Guy Fawkes lesen und verstehen. ○ ○ ○

Ich kann die Fragen zur Geschichte beantworten. ○ ○ ○

Ich kann das Lied „Bonfire Night" singen. ○ ○ ○

3 **Das weiß ich jetzt über Guy Fawkes:**
Hier ist Platz für deine Ideen. Du kannst alles aufschreiben, was du weißt, malen, Bilder aufkleben und beschriften usw.

Thanksgiving Day

1 **Diese Wörter kann ich benennen und aufschreiben:**
Hilfe findest du im Activity Book auf den Seiten 40 und 41 und im Pupil's Book auf Seite 39.

_____ _____ _____

_____ _____ _____

2 **Das weiß ich jetzt über Thanksgiving und die USA:**
Hier ist Platz für deine Ideen. Du kannst alles aufschreiben, was du weißt, malen, Bilder aufkleben und beschriften usw.

3 Das kann ich auch schon auf Englisch:

Ich kann die Geschichte von Carol's Thanksgiving verstehen.

Ich habe die „Story about the first Thanksgiving" verstanden und eigene Schriftzeichen dazu erfunden.

Ich kann das Lied „Wichi Tei" singen.

Ich kann ein Thanksgiving-Elfchen schreiben.

Christmas in Australia

1 **Diese Wörter kann ich benennen und aufschreiben:**
Hilfe findest du im Pupil's Book auf den Seiten 41 und 42.

_____   _____   _____

_____   _____   _____

2 **Das weiß ich jetzt über Australien:**
Hier ist Platz für deine Ideen. Du kannst alles aufschreiben, was du weißt, malen, Bilder aufkleben und beschriften usw.

3 Das kann ich auch schon auf Englisch:

Ich kann die Geschichte „Father Christmas in Australia" verstehen.
            ☐ ☐ ☐

Ich kann das Lied „The five days of Christmas" singen.   ☐ ☐ ☐

Ich habe den Text „Let's go to Australia" gehört
und kann die Sätze lesen und verstehen.   ☐ ☐ ☐

twenty-one 21

Easter

1 ✏️ **Diese Wörter kann ich benennen und aufschreiben:**
Hilfe findest du im Pupil's Book auf den Seiten 44 und 52.

 _____   _____

 _____   🌼 _____

Ich kann auf Englisch „Frohe Ostern" wünschen:

_____

2 Das hat mir beim Basteln der Osterkarte geholfen: ✓

☐ Ich habe die Anleitung im Pupil's Book mehrmals gelesen.

☐ Ich habe mir die Bilder genau angesehen.

☐ Wir haben uns in der Gruppe geholfen.

☐ _____

3 Das kann ich auch schon auf Englisch:

Ich kann das Lied „I like the flowers" singen.
                                                         ○ ○ ○
Ich kann noch ein anderes Osterlied singen
oder ein Gedicht aufsagen.   ○ ○ ○

4 ✏️ **Feedback**

Das hat mir in dieser Unit am meisten Spaß gemacht:

_____

Das hat mir nicht gefallen und das fand ich schwierig:

_____

22 twenty-two

Word fields

✎ **Hier sammle ich meine Lieblingswörter zu den verschiedenen Themen:**

Time and numbers	At home
Lunch	Hobbies and sports
Shopping	Transport

twenty-three 23

Word fields

Hier sammle ich meine Lieblingswörter zu den verschiedenen Themen: Im letzten Feld kannst du eine eigene Überschrift wählen.

Animals	At the doctor's

Scotland	Jobs

Special days	_____

Sally

Lehrwerk für den
Englischunterricht ab Klasse 3

Activity Book 4

Erarbeitet von
Martina Bredenbröcker
Daniela Elsner
Stefanie Gleixner-Weyrauch
Simone Gutwerk
Marion Lugauer

Unter Beratung von Jane Brockmann-Fairchild

Illustriert von
Monica May, Wilfried Poll,
Thilo Pustlauk und Gisela Vogel

Oldenbourg

Inhalt

Back to school 3

At home 7

Let's have lunch 12

My day 16

Hobbies and sports 19

Shopping 23

Jack and the beanstalk 26

Vehicles 27

Wild animals 31

At the doctor's 34

Going to Scotland 36

Jobs 38

Meeting people 39

Special days:

Thanksgiving Day 41

Schneidebogen 43

Back to school

Let's count!

💬 **1.** Find the differences. What's missing in picture number 2?

💬✏️ **2.** Complete the lists. Work with a partner and compare.

Picture number 1:

There are ____ computers.

There are _____ .

There are _____ .

There are _____ .

There are _____ .

There are _____ .

There are _____ .

There are _____ .

Picture number 2:

There is ____ computer.

There are _____ .

There are _____ .

There are _____ .

There are _____ .

There are _____ .

There are _____ .

There are _____ .

| chairs   pencils   pupils   rulers   tables   pens   schoolbags |

three 3

Back to school

Numbers

1. Cut out the puzzle (page 43), match the numbers and stick in.

two	four	nine	seven
six	eight	three	five
eleven	ten	twelve	one

2. Write down the numbers.

1 _____ 2 _____ 3 _____

4 _____ 5 _____ 6 _____

7 _____ 8 _____ 9 _____

10 _____ 11 _____ 12 _____

3. How much is it?

one + three = _____   seven + five = _____

two + six = _____   eight + three = _____

six + four = _____   nine + one = _____

4 four

Back to school

What time is it?

 1. Listen and number the clocks.

    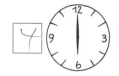

 2. Listen and tick ✔ the correct time.

Lunchtime!

 Back to school

The time

 1. Draw lines.

It's three o'clock.   It's twelve o'clock.   It's nine o'clock.

It's five o'clock.   It's eleven o'clock.   It's eight o'clock.

 2. Set the clock. Draw the clock's hands.

It's one o'clock.   It's eleven o'clock.   It's four o'clock.   It's seven o'clock.

 3. What time is it?

 It's _two o'clock_ .   _It's twelve o'clock_.

 It's six o'clock .   _It's nine o'clock_ .

 It's ten o'clock .   _It's eight o'clock_ .

 **At home**

Kangaroo's action rhyme

Kangaroo, kangaroo, _open the door_.

Kangaroo, kangaroo, _shake your head_.

 Kangaroo, kangaroo, _go to bed_.

Kangaroo, kangaroo, _touch the floor_.

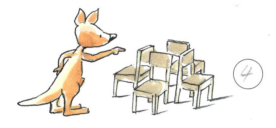 Kangaroo, kangaroo, _count the chairs_.

Kangaroo, kangaroo, _jump up the stairs_.

1. Number the pictures.

2. Write in the missing words.

> Kangaroo, kangaroo, open the door.
> Kangaroo, kangaroo, touch the floor.
> Kangaroo, kangaroo, jump up the stairs.
> Kangaroo, kangaroo, count the chairs.
> Kangaroo, kangaroo, shake your head.
> Kangaroo, kangaroo, go to bed.

seven **7**

At home

Rooms

✏️ **1.** Write down the names of the rooms.

_____   _____   _____

_____

| kitchen   bathroom   garden   bedroom   toilet   living room |

✏️ **2.** Where are the children? Find the correct answer. | Yes, he is. | Yes, she is. | No, he isn't. | No, she isn't. |

 Is Liz in the living room? _No, she isn't._

 Is Emily in the kitchen? _Yes, she is._

 Is Eric in the garden? _No, he isn't._

 Is Tim in the living room? _Yes, he is._

 Is Susan in the bathroom? _Yes, she is._

 Is Eric in the toilet? _Yes, he is._

 Is Phil in the garden? _No, he isn't._

 Is Emily in the bedroom? _No, she isn't._

 **At home**

Too big – too small

 1. Is it just right? Read, choose your answer, write and draw.

| Yes, it's just right. | No, it's too big. | No, it's too small. |

Is the bath just right for Susan?
No, it's too small.

Is the sofa just right for Tim?
_____

Is the bed just right for Phil?
_____

Is the chair just right for Liz?
_____

Is the door just right for Emily?
_____

2. Listen and number in the correct order.

- ③ just right
- ⑥ living room
- ① kitchen
- ⑤ garden
- ④ bedroom
- ② bathroom

nine 9

 **At home**

Furniture

 1. Count the pieces of furniture and colour them.
Work with a partner and compare.

There are __3__ beds.   There are __6__ stereos.

There are __3__ tables.   There are __3__ chairs.

There are __4__ shelves.   There are __6__ lamps.

There are __2__ cupboards.   There are __2__ sofas.

There are __4__ desks.

2. Do the crossword.

bed   chair   window
table   desk   sofa   cupboard
shelves   stereo   lamp

My home is my castle!

10 ten

At home

Susan's room

1. Cut out the furniture (page 43). Listen and stick the furniture in.

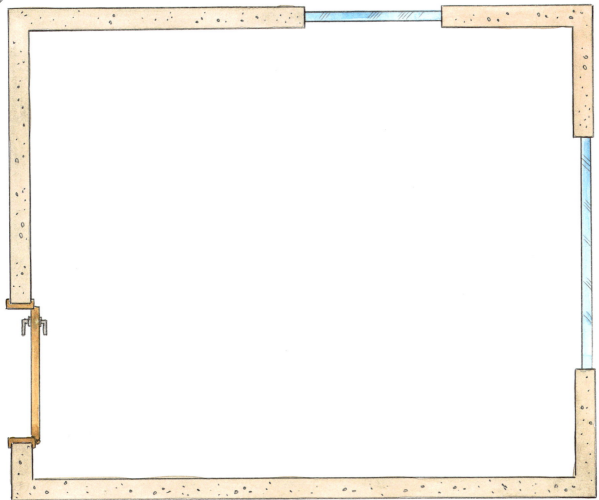

2. Complete the sentences. Read your text to your group.

The bed is under the _____.

The sofa is _____.

The desk is _____.

The cupboard is _____.

The lamp is _____.

The shelves are between the _____ and the _____.

in front of   next to   behind   under
bed   small window   door   sofa   big window   desk

Let's have lunch

Let's make a sandwich!

1. Find the words and circle ○ them.

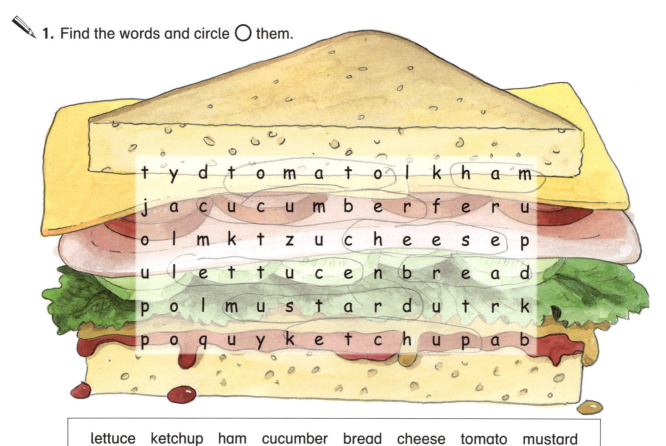

| lettuce | ketchup | ham | cucumber | bread | cheese | tomato | mustard |

2. Draw your own sandwich. Write down what you put in it.

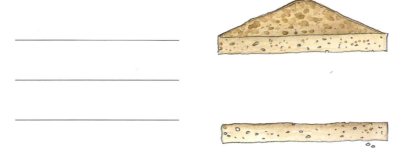

3. Listen to the song and tick ✓ the correct sandwich.

The sandwich is made out of: _____

12 twelve

Let's have lunch

It's time for lunch!

1. Read the menu.

Monday
1 tomato soup
2 salad with cheese

Tuesday
1 sausage with mashed potatoes
2 carrot soup

Wednesday
1 fish and chips
2 ham sandwich

Thursday
1 spaghetti
2 cheese sandwich

Friday
1 salad with ham
2 pizza

2. Write your own menu plan. Tell your partner.

Monday: _____

Tuesday: _____

Wednesday: _____

Thursday: _____

Friday: _____

3. In the dining hall: Listen and match.

Monday

Tuesday

Wednesday

Thursday

Friday

4. Listen again. What's missing? Draw.

thirteen 13

Let's have lunch

Let's lay the table!

1. Lay the table for eight people. Count and draw.

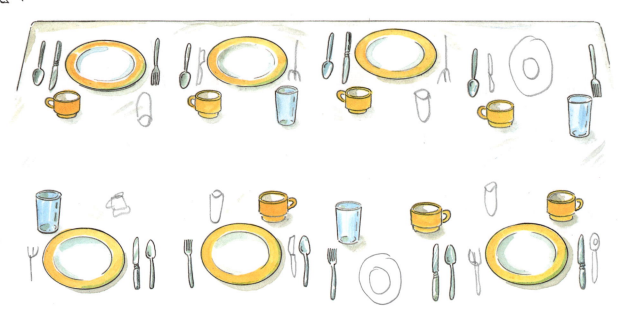

2. What's missing? Complete the sentence and read it to your partner.

_4_ forks, _2_ plates, _3_ knives, _1_ cup, _1_ spoon, _4_ glasses are missing.

3. Which answer is correct? Write it down.

You eat soup with it: It's a _spoon_.

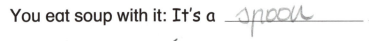

You need it for cutting: It's a _knife_.

You put lemonade in it: It's a _glass_.

You eat from it: It's a _plate_.

You pick up food with it: It's a _fork_.

You drink tea out of it: It's a _cup_.

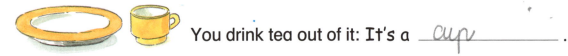

14 fourteen

Let's have lunch

In the restaurant

1. Listen and complete the speech bubbles.

2. Make up the dialogue. Write it down.

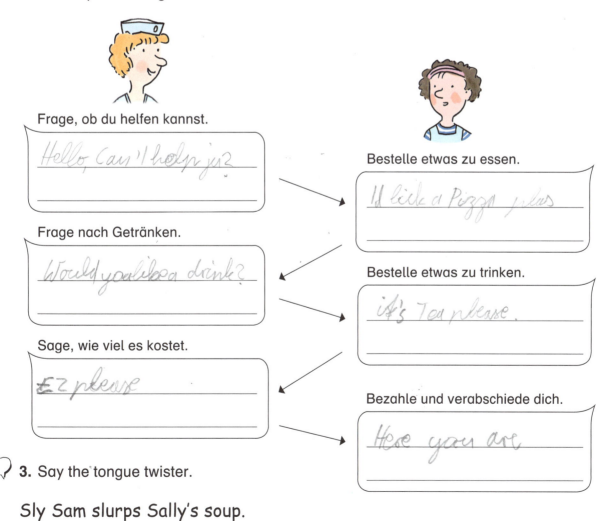

3. Say the tongue twister.

Sly Sam slurps Sally's soup.

My day

Through the day

 1. Listen to the song.

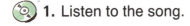 2. Cut out the text (page 45), match and stick it in.

 3. Set the clock. Draw the clock's hands.

Hickory, dickory, dock!
The mouse ran up the clock.
The clock struck one.
The mouse ran down.
Hickory, dickory, dock!

My day

One day in the life of Alpha 72

At 3 o'clock
I _____ .

At 4 o'clock
I have _____ .

At 5 o'clock
I _____ my hair.

At 6 o'clock
I _____ .
We _____ to fly.

At 10 o'clock
I have _____ .

At 1 o'clock
I _____ .

At 2 o'clock
I _____ with my pet.

At 4 o'clock
I _____ my friends.

At 6 o'clock
I _____ .

| learn | go to bed | get up | brush | go to school | breakfast |
| call | lunch | do my homework | play | | |

1. Listen.

2. Cut out the pictures (page 45), match and stick them in.

3. Write in the missing words.

My day

My day

  **in the morning**

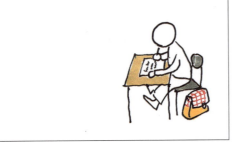

  **in the afternoon**

  **in the evening/at night**

1. What's your day like? Write and draw.

2. Tell your class about your day.

>   get up
>   learn at school   have lunch
>   play (ball) with my friends
>   go to bed and sleep

Hobbies and sports

What's your hobby?

1. Draw lines.

swimming
riding a mountain bike
playing the guitar
reading books
ice skating
playing the piano
snowboarding
playing football
riding a horse

2. Complete the sentences.

 Susan likes *riding a horse*.

Tim likes *playing the piano*

and _____.

 Emily likes *reading books*

and _____.

Eric likes *playing the guitar*.

 Phil likes *snowboarding*

 and _____.

Liz likes *swimming*.

nineteen 19

Hobbies and sports

This is me!

1. Listen. Write in the missing words.

Hi, my _____ is Will.

I'm _____ years old.

I _____ in Chester.

I'm in _____ 4f.

My _____ are football and

playing _____ .

Hello, my _____ is Jenny.

I'm _____ years old.

I _____ in Chester, too.

I'm in _____ 5d.

My hobbies are _____ and

playing _____ .

> name   ten   eleven   class   live
> computer games   singing   basketball   hobbies

2. Draw a picture of yourself or stick in a photo.

3. Write about yourself. Read your text to your class.

Hi, my name is _____

_____

_____

_____

_____

20 twenty

Hobbies and sports

An interview with a sports star

Do your own interview, write it down and act it out.
Work with a partner.

Begrüße den Sportstar und frage,
wie es ihm/ihr geht.

Sage, wie es dir geht.

Frage, ob er/sie
Volleyball spielen kann.

Bejahe.

Frage, ob er/sie auch
Klavier spielen kann.

Verneine.

Bedanke dich für das Interview.

Hobbies and sports

The sporty rap

 1. Listen to the rap.

 2. Write in the missing words.

The sporty rap

I do it. It's ___okay___ .

I like it when I ___play___ .

I do it. It's ___fun___ .

I like it when I ___run___ .

I do it. It's ___great___ .

I like it when I ___skate___ .

Playing, running, skating, riding after ___shool___ ?

Yes, we ___like___ it!

Yes, we ___love___ it!

Yes, we ___do___ !

| skate | fun | okay | run | great | play |
| school | | do | love | like | |

 3. Read the skipping rhymes.

Apples, peaches, pears and plums,
tell me when your birthday comes.
January, February, March …

I like coffee, I like tea,
I like Sally to jump with me.
One, two, three …

Teddy bear, teddy bear, turn around.
Teddy bear, teddy bear, touch the ground.
Teddy bear, teddy bear, show your shoe.
Teddy bear, teddy bear, that will do!
Teddy bear, teddy bear, go upstairs.
Teddy bear, teddy bear, say your prayers.
Teddy bear, teddy bear, turn out the light.
Teddy bear, teddy bear, say good night!

22 twenty-two

Shopping

In the supermarket

1. Complete Sally's shopping list. Draw lines.

Sally's shopping list:
bread
eggs
milk
cheese
spinach
ice cream
biscuits
chocolate bars
lemonade
lollipops

2. Listen and tick ✔.

Phil's shopping list:

3. Write Phil's shopping list.

Shopping

At the shopping centre

1. Listen and tick ✔ the correct answer.

The girls want a CD by	the Supergirls. ☐	Eric and Phil go to	the supermarket. ☐
	the Fantastic Girls. ☐		the toy shop. ☐
	the Superboys. ☐		the book shop. ☐

Liz needs	a new jacket. ☐	The girls go to	the cinema. ☐
	a T-shirt. ☐		the book shop. ☐
	socks. ☐		the sports shop. ☐

2. Listen. Cut out the speech bubbles (page 45), match and stick them in.

24 twenty-four

Shopping

In the shop

Make up the dialogue. Write it down.

Frage, ob du dem Kunden helfen kannst.

Sage, was du kaufen möchtest.

Zeige dem Kunden die Ware.
Biete ihm an, sie anzuprobieren.

Bedanke dich.

Sage, dass dir das Kleidungsstück passt/gefällt. Frage, wie viel es kostet.

Nenne den Preis.

Bezahle.

Bedanke dich und verabschiede dich.

Verabschiede dich.

pullover, socks, boots, sweatshirt, jacket, jeans, T-shirt, shoes

It's perfect.
I like it.

Jack and the beanstalk

 1. Listen to the story.

 2. Cut out the pictures (page 47), match and stick them in.

 3. Cut out the speech bubbles (page 47), match and stick them in.

 4. What fairy tales do you know? Show your books in class.

Vehicles

Detective Brighthead

1. Find the words.

traintaxistationcarferrybusunderground

 2. Listen and draw Detective Brighthead's way.

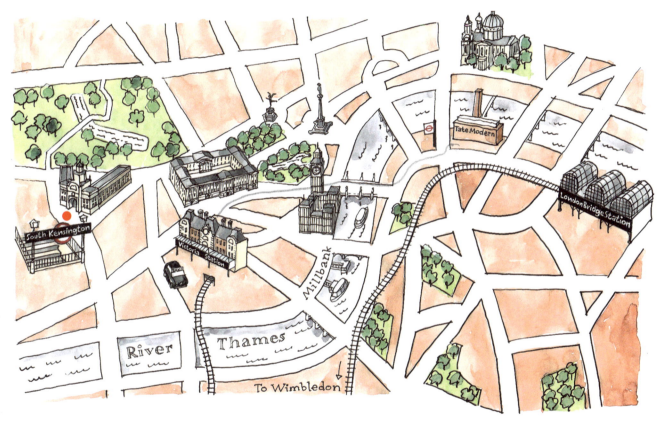

3. Complete the words.

__ __ain to London

b__ __ to London Bridge

__ __derground day card £5

The ticket is for the _____

The ticket is for the _____

The ticket is for the _____

twenty-seven 27

Vehicles

Follow Detective Brighthead's way

Read the story and find the right way.
Circle ○ the correct answers.
Your book can help you.

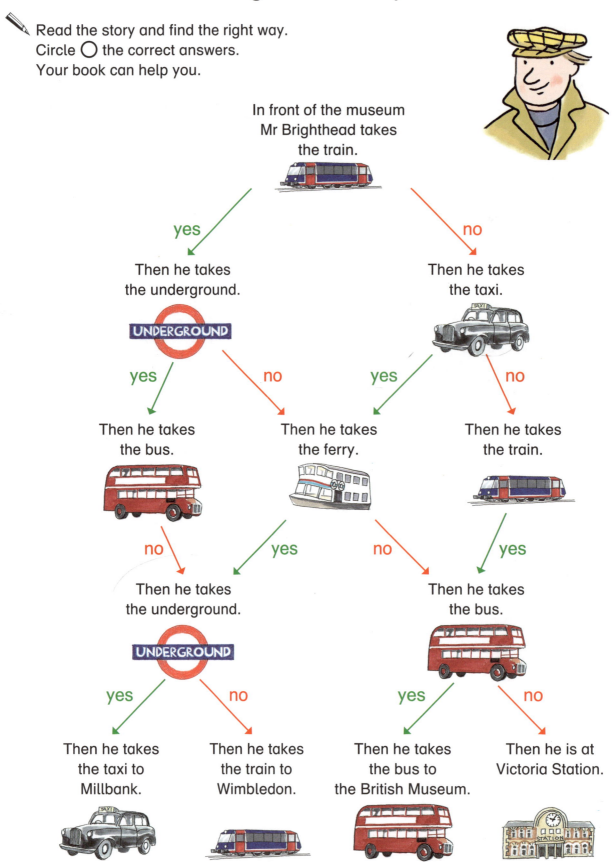

Vehicles

On the way

 1. Listen and follow the grey route.

You arrive in _____ .

 2. Listen and find your way.

route 1: You arrive _____ .

route 2: You arrive _____ .

3. Listen and draw lines.

Fasten your seat belts, please!

No smoking!

Put your seats in an upright position!

Switch off your mobile phones, radios and laptops!

Vehicles

Vehicles

Look at the picture and complete the sentences.

 Susan is going by __ferry__.

 Phil is going by __underground__.

 Mr Brighthead __is going by plane__.

 Liz __is going by taxi__.

 Eric __is going by train__.

 Tim __is going by bus__.

Emily __is going by car__.

| plane | ferry | car | bus | underground | train | taxi |

30 thirty

Wild animals

Animals of the wild

1. Read and draw lines.

monkey

elephant

tortoise

lion

strong

clever

big

funny

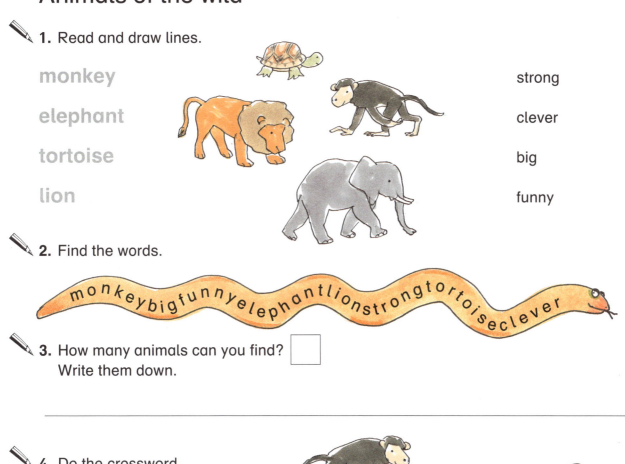

2. Find the words.

3. How many animals can you find? ☐
Write them down.

4. Do the crossword.

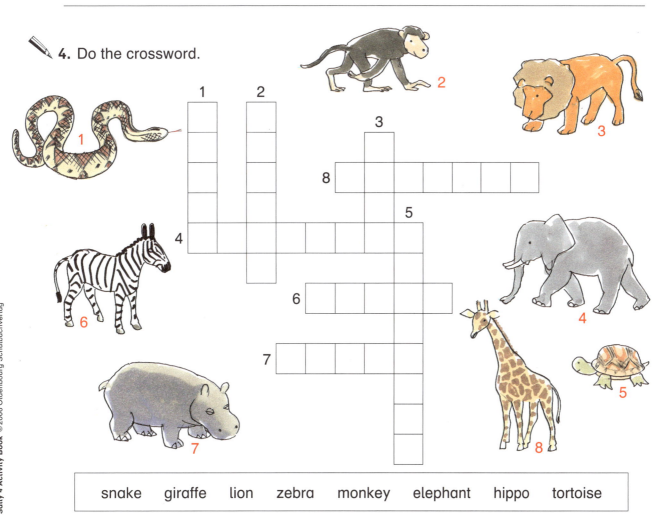

snake   giraffe   lion   zebra   monkey   elephant   hippo   tortoise

thirty-one 31

Wild animals

Detective Brighthead's trip to the jungle

1. Crazy photos! Which animal is it?
Number and write.

Wild animals

snake [5]   [1] [2]   [6] hippo

tortoise [7]   [3] [4]   [2] giraffe

lion [3]   [5] [6]   [8] monkey

zebra [1]   [7] [8]   [4] elephant

2. Crazy animals! What's wrong?

The __tortoise__ is too __fast__ .

The __monkey__ is too __strong__ .

The __zebra__ is too __clever__ .

The __giraffe__ is too __small__ .

The __lion__ is too __fat__ .

| fat | clever | strong | small | fast |

3. Write word cards for an animal bingo.

32 thirty-two

Wild animals

Walking through the jungle

1. Listen to the song. Write in the missing words.

1. Walking through the 🌴 _jungel_ , guess what I see?

   I can see an 🐘 _elefant_ waving to me.

2. I can see a tall 🦒 _____ looking down at me.

3. I can see a 🦛 _____ swimming in the sea.

4. I can see a 🦓 _____ running fast to me.

5. I can see a 🐒 _____ climbing in a tree.

   Can you go on?   I can see _____

   _____ .

The clever tortoise

2. Listen and tick ✔: yes or no?

	yes	no
The tortoise, the monkey and the snake live in Africa.	☐	☐
One day there is a big party.	☐	☐
The zebra is the king of the jungle.	☐	☐
The clever tortoise has got an idea.	☐	☐
The hippo and the elephant play tennis.	☐	☐
The tortoise plays a trick on the elephant and the hippo.	☐	☐

At the doctor's

At the doctor's

1. Number and write the words.

   1 headache
   2 neckache
   3 earache
   4 backache

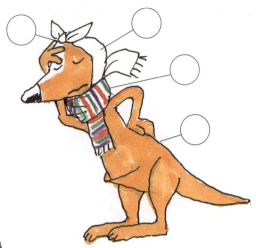

2. Complete the speech bubbles.

I'm sick.

My _____ hurts.

I've got an _____ .

I'm sick.

My _____ _____ .

I've got a _____ .

I'm _____ .

My _____ _____ .

I've got a _____ .

_____

_____

_____

_____

| neck | ear | back | head | headache |
| backache | earache | neckache |

34 thirty-four

At the doctor's

The inline skating accident

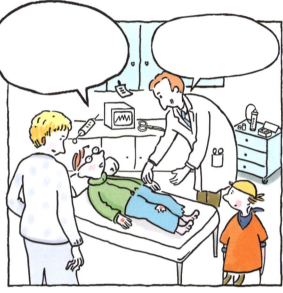

Listen. Cut out the speech bubbles (page 47), match and stick them in.

Going to Scotland

In Scotland

1. Where is Nessie? Write in: behind, under, in.

Nessie is _____ the boat.   Nessie is _____ Sally.   Nessie is _____ the lake.

2. Draw your own Nessie monster. Show your picture to your group.

3. Write the correct words under the pictures.

_____   _____   _____

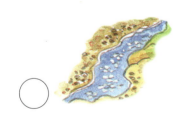  

_____   _____   _____

river   mountain   lake   sea   Highland Games   castle

1 on Monday   2 on Tuesday   3 on Wednesday   4 on Thursday   5 on Friday

4. Listen, match the days of the week and number.

36 thirty-six

Going to Scotland

A trip to Scotland

1. Listen and number the Browns' route.

2. Find Nessie on the map. Nessie is _____.

3. Draw a tartan pattern. Show it to your group.

 Jobs

Eric's jobs

1. Complete the sentences.

I _____ .   Monday

I _____ .   Tuesday

I _____ .   Wednesday

I _____ .   Thursday

I _____ .   Friday

I _____ .   Saturday

I _____ .   Sunday

| make my bed   tidy my room   feed the cat   walk the dog |
| help in the kitchen   do my homework   help in the garden |

 2. Listen, match the days of the week and draw lines. Which day is left over?

Meeting people

My cat likes to hide in boxes

1. Where are these cats from? Draw lines and write.

Germany
Greece
Japan
France
Spain

2. Complete the sentences.

Cat number 1 is from _____.

Cat number 2 is _____.

Cat number 3 _____.

Cat number 4 _____.

Cat number 5 _____.

3. And this is my cat:

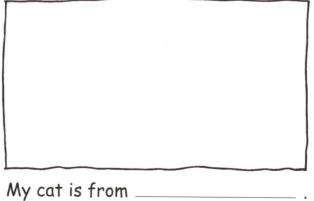

England
Italy
Poland
Turkey
Russia
USA
...

My cat is from _____.

4. Show your picture to your group.

thirty-nine 39

Meeting people

Looking for a penfriend

My name is Emily.
I'm ten. I'm a girl.
I live in England.
My hobby is reading books.
I'm looking for a penfriend (girl)
from Germany. Age 10.

1. Fill in.

This is me: name: _____

boy/girl   country: _____

age: _____

hobby: _____

I'm looking for: boy/girl   country: _____

age: _____

2. And what are you looking for? Read your text to your class.

This is me: name: _____

boy/girl   country: _____

age: _____

I'm looking for: boy/girl   country: _____

age: _____

My hobbies are _____

_____.

I can speak _____.

40 forty

Thanksgiving Day

Let's be thankful!

 1. Listen, colour and speak.   red, pink, blue, black,
The apples are …   green, orange, grey,
yellow, white, brown

2. Draw lines.

apples   oranges   cherries   lemons

plums   pears

tomatoes   corn

potatoes   carrots   beans

 3. What are you thankful for? Write it down.

I'm thankful for

Corn on the cob

Prepare the cob.
Boil it for 5 to 10 minutes.
Serve it with butter and salt.
Enjoy your meal!

 4. What happens on Carol's Thanksgiving Day? Read and draw lines.

In the evening   we go to the Thanksgiving parade.
In the morning   we watch the football match on TV.
In the afternoon   my mum puts the turkey into the oven.

forty-one 41

Thanksgiving Day

A story about the first Thanksgiving

Little Bear   sees   a ship.

Little Bear   sees   some white people.

The Indians help   the white people   to build their houses,   to plant corn,

to hunt turkeys   and to catch fish.

The Indians   and the white people   have a big party:

the first Thanksgiving.

 1. Write the story in your own Indian signs. Show it to your group.

2. Find out and learn about the American Indians in the internet.

Schneidebogen

✂ Numbers (page 4)

✂ Susan's room (page 11)

Schneidebogen

✂ Through the day (page 16)

At eight o'clock in the morning
I get up and eat.
I have some milk and some cornflakes
with sugar – so it's sweet.

At three o'clock in the afternoon
school is over – hooray!
I go home and watch TV,
have fun with my friends and play.

At nine o'clock in the morning
I'm already at school.
I learn till I hear the bell ring
for lunchtime and that's cool.

At eight o'clock in the evening
I read and go to bed.
Then I turn all the lights off
and say: "Good night!" to Mum and Dad.

✂ One day in the life of Alpha 72 (page 17)

✂ At the shopping centre (page 24)

It's too big.
It's £25.
Here are the jackets. Try them on.
It's perfect.
How much is it?
Hello. Can I help you?
Yes, please. I'd like a new jacket.
Here you are.
Thank you.
Thank you. Goodbye.

Schneidebogen

✂ Jack and the beanstalk (page 26)

| Here are five magic beans for your cow. | We must sell the cow. | I must climb it. |
| Now we can buy a new cow! | A castle, a kitchen and an apple pie. Yummy! | |

✂ The inline skating accident (page 35)

| What's the matter? | Ready, steady, go! | Let's go to the doctor's. | Next, please. | Your leg is broken. |
| My leg hurts so much. And my hand hurts, too. | Your hand is not broken. Put some ice on it. | | | |